# BOOK ANALYSIS

Written by Hadrien Seret
and Margot Pépin
Translated by Soline de Dorlodot
and Rebecca Neal

# A Bag of Marbles
BY JOSEPH JOFFO

Bright
≡Summaries.com

**BOOK ANALYSIS**

# Shed new light
# on your favorite books with

Bright
≡**Summaries**.com

**www.brightsummaries.com**

| | |
|---|---|
| **JOSEPH JOFFO** | 9 |
| ***A BAG OF MARBLES*** | 13 |
| **SUMMARY** | 17 |

  The dangers of being Jewish
  The journey to the free zone
  Arrival in Menton
  Escape to Nice
  The end of the war and the Liberation

| | |
|---|---|
| **CHARACTER STUDY** | 25 |

  Joseph Joffo
  Maurice Joffo
  Henri and Albert Joffo
  The parents

| | |
|---|---|
| **ANALYSIS** | 33 |

  Historical context
  An autobiographical novel
  A child's-eye view of the war
  A story of hope and fear

| | |
|---|---|
| **FURTHER REFLECTION** | 51 |
| **FURTHER READING** | 55 |

# JOSEPH JOFFO

## FRENCH WRITER

- **Born in Paris in 1931.**
- **Notable works:**
  - *A Bag of Marbles* (1973), novel
  - *Baby-foot* (1977), novel
  - *Tendre été* ("Tender Summer", 1981), novel

Joseph Joffo is a French author of Jewish descent, and was born in 1931. He initially worked as a hairdresser, before taking up writing to exorcise the demons of a childhood shaped by the Second World War (1939-1945) and the Holocaust. This exercise in introspection resulted in *A Bag of Marbles*, which quickly became an international bestseller.

His work is mostly autobiographical, although he has also written some works of fiction, including *Anna and her Orchestra* (1975), which is loosely based on his mother's life, and *Le Cavalier de la Terre Promise* ("The Knight from the Promised Land", 1983), as well as short stories such as

*Bashert* (2009).

It is worth noting that Joffo's writing process involves producing a first draft himself before using a ghostwriter to polish the text. This means that the final, published books are not purely his own work.

# *A BAG OF MARBLES*

## A JEWISH CHILD'S JOURNEY DURING THE SECOND WORLD WAR

- **Genre:** autobiographical novel
- **Reference edition:** Joffo, J. (2001) *A Bag of Marbles*. Trans. Sokolinsky, M. Chicago: University of Chicago Press.
- **1st edition:** 1973
- **Themes:** hope, anti-Semitism, Occupation, Holocaust, solidarity, brotherhood

*A Bag of Marbles* is an autobiographical novel by Joseph Joffo. It was first published in 1973 and is set between 1941 and 1944, when France was occupied by German forces. It is his best-known book, having sold several million copies to date and been translated into 18 languages.

The novel is a lively, dynamic account of the author and his brother Maurice's adventures as they fled the Nazis during the Vichy regime (1940-1944). Their journey features both carefree and happy periods, and more difficult moments of danger and imprisonment.

*A Bag of Marbles* forms part of a trilogy of autobiographical novels depicting Joffo's childhood, and is its second instalment from a chronological perspective. *Agates et Calots* (1997) is set before the events of *A Bag of Marbles*, while *Baby-foot* describes his adolescence after the war.

# SUMMARY

## THE DANGERS OF BEING JEWISH

The story begins in 1941 in Paris. In the Jewish neighbourhood of Clignancourt, Maurice and Joseph Joffo are playing with marbles. After an exuberant game, the two brothers head home to the apartment above their father's hair salon. They stand in front of the window, concealing the sign that indicates that it is a Jewish establishment, and look on as two SS men go in. The atmosphere is tense as they get their hair cut, and when they are about to leave, the boys' father tells them that the man who just cut their hair is a Jew and all the other customers are Jewish.

Shortly afterwards, a decree is passed forcing all Jews to wear a yellow star, so Maurice and Joseph's mother sews one onto their jackets. This new emblem does not go unnoticed: at school, the boys can see that their teachers are uncomfortable, and at breaktime some of the other children hurl racist epithets at them or even hit them. However, Joseph manages to swap his star for his friend Zérati's bag of marbles.

As even harsher discriminatory measures targeting Jews are introduced, Joseph's father orders his two sons to travel to the free zone to join their brothers Albert and Henri in Menton (southeastern France), where they will be safe. During the trip, they will have to be constantly on their guard and conceal the fact that they are Jewish. Their parents will take another route and join them later.

## THE JOURNEY TO THE FREE ZONE

Maurice and Joseph head to the Gare d'Austerlitz to take a train to Dax (southwestern France), carrying bags filled with their possessions and 10 000 francs, but no identification papers. The journey is long and difficult, the train is packed and the children are hungry. Once they arrive, the two boys start to panic as they notice that two SS officers are about to check their carriage. Fortunately, one of their fellow travellers, a priest, takes them under his protection and saves them from being arrested.

They then arrive in the village of Hagetmau,

where they are left with barely enough money to get into the free zone after paying for a paltry meal. They spend their last 1000 francs on the crossing, and the young smuggler who takes them across the border leads them to a farm, where a farmer is letting exhausted refugees stay and get some sleep.

Maurice was paying attention to the route they took on the way over, which allows him to smuggle some other refugees across during the night. He makes 20 000 francs, which is enough to take care of their needs for some time. The next day, they walk for hours before a man invites them to ride in his carriage to Aire-sur-Adour, where they then take a train to Marseille.

In Marseille, the two brothers see the sea for the first time and discover Nazi propaganda at the cinema. As they set off again, they narrowly escape the clutches of two policemen who seem suspicious of them. Joseph pretends that a total stranger is his father to throw them off; this will not be the last time the boys' guile and resourcefulness gets them out of trouble.

## ARRIVAL IN MENTON

Finally, they meet up with Albert and Henri in sunny Menton, where the two older brothers have managed to land work as hairdressers. For a few days, the children make the most of the fine weather, the beach, games like football, and the new friends they make. However, they soon have to look for work to cover the family's expenses. Maurice is hired by a bakery, while Joseph works for a farmer named Monsieur Viale up in the mountains and spends time with his wife, a former aristocrat with a keen interest in music, books and chess.

One day, on his way back to Menton, Joseph learns from Albert that their parents have been arrested in a raid and are being held at the stadium in Pau (southwestern France). Henri leaves to attempt to secure their release, and in the meantime the two younger brothers are sent to school. One week later, Henri comes back with good news: their parents have been freed and have gone to Nice. However, their joy is short-lived: Albert and Henri are called up to work in Germany, which forces the brothers to flee to Nice.

## ESCAPE TO NICE

In Nice, the children and their parents are finally all back together under the same roof. Maurice and Joseph prove particularly resourceful, and are well-liked by most of the Italian soldiers staying in Nice. Alongside their schoolwork, they make a tidy sum of money on the black market. However, in 1943 Italy surrenders and is occupied by the Allies, which means that the Italian soldiers leave France to fight and are replaced by Germans. The family is forced to split up once more, and the two brothers set off again.

Maurice and Joseph follow their father's advice and go to New Harvest, an education camp ostensibly run by the Vichy government which is actually sheltering Jewish children. There, they learn to cook and lead a peaceful life. However, during a ride out to Nice with the camp's driver, they are arrested and taken to the SS headquarters at the Hôtel Excelsior.

The two brothers are separated and interrogated several times, but thanks to a plan they came up with in advance, they both manage to pass themselves off as French Catholics from Algeria. They are also unexpectedly helped by a Jewish doctor, who claims that they were circumcised for medical reasons. They are kept at the hotel for seven days while the Nazis decide what to do with them, during which time Joseph falls ill and becomes delirious.

The new head of the Excelsior issues them with an ultimatum: if they do not produce baptism certificates within two days, they will be deported. Maurice manages to obtain the documents from a priest, whose efforts on their behalf secure their freedom.

Back at New Harvest, the two brothers learn that their father has been arrested during a raid. This is the last they ever hear of him. They know that they are in danger and go to Montluçon, where they are taken in by their sister Rosette. However, she knows that someone there is denouncing hidden Jews, so she sends them on to the village of R., where she hopes that they will be safer.

# THE END OF THE WAR AND THE LIBERATION

Maurice and Joseph spend 1943 and 1944 in R., where Joseph delivers newspapers and works in a bookshop owned by Monsieur Mancelier, an anti-Semite and staunch supporter of Marshal Pétain. He also helps the local Resistance. Meanwhile, Maurice works in a restaurant, and the two boys earn a little extra on the side by forging rationing coupons. Some time later, Paris is liberated and the Germans leave France. While R. is swept up in the euphoria of victory, Joseph seizes the opportunity to go back to the capital. Maurice soon follows him, but not before getting his hands on some reblochon cheese to sell in Paris.

Over the course of the war, Joseph has left his childhood behind. In Paris, the Joffo family are reunited in their hairdressing salon in Clignancourt, but their father is not with them, and they soon realise that he will not be coming back.

# CHARACTER STUDY

## JOSEPH JOFFO

He is the author, narrator and main character of the autobiography.

When the story begins in 1941, he is a ten-year-old Jewish boy, and although he is a good student, he is terrible at marbles. He is intellectually curious, and devours the few books that he comes across during his journey.

He struggles to adapt to his forced exile and constant travelling. During the early stages of their journey to Menton, he relies entirely on his brother's common sense and does not make any decisions himself, preferring to simply follow Maurice.

However, his travels through France and Italy help him to grow up and make him less childlike and naive. He becomes tougher, both physically ("Now I can walk for hours without getting blisters. The soles of my feel, the skin of my heels have hardened") and mentally ("I wonder if I am still a child... I doubt if playing jacks or marbles would appeal to me now [...]. But these things do belong to my age; after all, I'm not quite twelve years old. They should excite me... but they don't").

People are naturally sympathetic to him, and this helps him on his journey (for example, he receives preferential treatment at Tite's café in Nice). Over the course of the story he also develops a practical intelligence which gets him out of a few scrapes (for example, he escapes two policemen at Marseille train station by asking a passer-by for the time and pretending to be his son).

These qualities, as well as sheer luck, save him from the Nazis and allow him to return to Paris unscathed after the Liberation.

## MAURICE JOFFO

Maurice is two years older than Joseph. He is impulsive, rowdy, shrewd and courageous. In *A Bag of Marbles*, he quickly becomes Joseph's protector during their journey.

Indeed, until their arrival in Menton, Maurice is the one who steers them around obstacles and leads them to safety: he makes a tidy sum by smuggling refugees into the free zone, puts Joseph's ideas into practice, and takes care of him by waking him up on the train. He is also the one who makes up the story about their Algerian origins and gets his hands on the baptism certificates that they need to escape from the SS at the Hôtel Excelsior in Nice.

He is also enterprising and quick to adapt to new circumstances: he works as a smuggler and lands jobs in a bakery and a restaurant, as well as arranging work on the side so that the brothers can earn extra money. He is lively, intelligent and protective, and accompanies Joseph throughout the story, sharing his struggles and providing him with unstinting support.

He returns to Paris shortly after his younger brother, and has also been changed by the three years of hardship and danger.

# HENRI AND ALBERT JOFFO

Henri and Albert are Joseph and Maurice's two older brothers, and have followed in their father's footsteps by becoming hairdressers and working in the family's salon on the rue Clignancourt. During the Occupation, they move to Menton in the free zone to escape persecution for being Jewish.

The two brothers are resourceful, sociable and naturally cheerful, and these qualities help them to adapt to the myriad changes that the war brings: in Menton, they work in a hair salon and soon become well-known and well-liked in the town, while in Nice they cut affluent clients' hair in their homes ("This one is a fancy salon, the most popular in Nice, and Henri and Albert often make house calls for hair-styling in some luxurious apartment or in a suite at the Majestic or the Negresco").

They are daring and courageous, and live by the principle that they always "have to try something", no matter how hopeless the situation may seem. For example, when they find out that their parents have been arrested by the Gestapo, they are prepared to go to any lengths to try and secure their release: Henri goes to Paris to negotiate with the Gestapo and somehow manages to convince the Nazis that they have made a mistake. Thanks to this risky endeavour, their parents are released a week later and Henri returns to Menton safe and sound.

The two brothers' resourcefulness and quick thinking enables them to emerge from the war unscathed. After the Liberation, they go back to Paris and take over their father's salon.

## THE PARENTS

Joseph's parents are originally from Russia, but had to flee the country because of anti-Jewish pogroms. They both came to France, where they met each other and started a family.

Having already experienced religious persecution, they are very aware of the risks facing them under the Vichy regime and are quick to take action. Their priority is to protect their children, which is why they make the painful decision to send them to the free zone unaccompanied. This allows them to save their family, but they are arrested in a raid in Pau. They are subsequently released, thanks to both Henri's bold manoeuvring and his mother's false papers, which claim that she is a descendant of the Romanovs (the ruling dynasty in Russia until the Revolution in 1917).

Joseph's father's luck runs out the second time he is arrested, and he is deported to a concentration camp. He never comes back, and the author comments: "In the end, Hitler turned out to be crueler than the Czar".

# ANALYSIS

## HISTORICAL CONTEXT

The dialogue and descriptions in *A Bag of Marbles* contain many references to the historical context. Although they are not strictly essential to the story, they give the reader a better understanding of the stakes at play in the story and its broader setting. This section will explain some of the key moments in the war and in the escalating persecution of the Jews.

### The rise of Hitler and Nazi ideology

1934 was a difficult year in Germany: the country had not recovered from its defeat in the First World War, and had been hit hard by the Great Depression that had begun in 1929. That year, Adolf Hitler, who had previously launched a failed coup, was elected chancellor. He quickly established an authoritarian regime underpinned by Nazi ideology, which claimed that the so-called "Germanic race" was superior to all others and that the Jews were responsible for all the evils of the world.

His goal was to create a vast empire free of anyone who, in his view, could weaken the German nation, namely individuals with physical or mental disabilities, homosexuals, Romani and Jews. To do this, he created the Gestapo, a secret police force tasked with eliminating the opponents to the regime, and the SS, whose main role was to organise the deportation and extermination of Jews. We get a glimpse of the SS's cruelty when Joseph and Maurice are held at the Hôtel Excelsior. Hitler also oversaw the establishment of extermination camps, which claimed millions of victims during the Second World War.

## The defeat of France and the Vichy government

In order to make these ambitions a reality, Germany invaded Austria, Poland and Czechoslovakia in 1939, triggering the outbreak of the Second World War. Although France initially fought alongside the Allies against the Germans, it surrendered a year later, in June 1940. This led to the establishment of the Vichy government, led by General Philippe Pétain (1856-1951), a hero of the First World War. France was partitioned into a free zone in the south and an occupied zone in the north. French Jews were persecuted under the Occupation (1940-1944), which is why the Joffos left Paris for the free zone in the south.

The Vichy regime followed a policy of total collaboration with the Germans. Specifically, a large number of Jews were deported to the concentration camps, and young French citizens were sent to Germany as part of the *Service du travail obligatoire* ("Compulsory Work Service"). In the novel, Albert and Henri are summoned to work in Germany, but they opt to flee to Nice instead.

Joffo illustrates the two main reactions of French citizens: they chose either collaboration (Mancelier, who owns a bookshop in R., admires Marshal Pétain and holds deeply anti-Semitic beliefs) or resistance, which could be active (Monsieur Jean, a member of the Resistance in R., the priest at the church of La Buffa in Nice, and Monsieur Subinagui, the director of New Harvest) or passive (the Viale family, who give Joseph work on their remote farm in the mountains).

## Anti-Jewish discrimination: the yellow star and the raids

From 1942 onwards, the Nazi regime began forcing Jews in Germany to sew a yellow fabric star onto their clothing, and the Vichy government adopted a similar policy in France. This star made it easier to identify Jews and enforce the restrictions imposed on them: for example, Jewish citizens could not practise certain jobs, were subject to strict rationing and were banned from attending ordinary schools.

This new law convinces Joseph's father to send his children to the free zone. He tells Joseph and Maurice: "You've seen that the Germans are getting harder with us all the time. There was the census they took, the notice stuck on the shop window; today there was the yellow star, tomorrow we'll be arrested. So we've got to run".

His comments prove prescient, as the Vichy government began deporting Jews to the death camps shortly afterwards. To capture the Jews, the German and French police usually organised raids. These operations, which varied in scale, aimed to arrest the people living in a particular area. Once their identities had been checked, all the Jews and anyone suspected of belonging to an "undesirable" group were imprisoned. After one such raid, Joseph's father was deported to a camp, where he later died.

The Jews could also be incarcerated because they had been denounced by someone else. This is why Joseph and Maurice's sister Rosette cannot take them in: with a heavy heart, she explains "There's an informer in the village".

## AN AUTOBIOGRAPHICAL NOVEL

### The autobiographical pact

*A Bag of Marbles* in an autobiographical novel, which means that the author, narrator and main character are all the same person. It is written in the first person and the author recounts his own experiences, which results in a highly subjective narrative. As Joffo himself explains, in writing the novel he has "drawn on [his] childhood recollections to tell [his] adventures during the Occupation", when he was ten years old.

In any autobiographical work, there is what the

French academic Philippe Lejeune has referred to as the "autobiographical pact" between the reader and the author-narrator (*Le Pacte autobiographique*, 1975). According to the terms of this tacit pact, the author has a duty to tell the truth and be sincere. In the prologue to the French edition of the novel, Joffo refers to this pact by evoking the "authenticity" of the narrative that follows, although he concedes that the 30 years that have elapsed since these events took place mean that some details may not be wholly accurate.

## A duty to remember

Although Joffo has always claimed that his book is not the work of a historian, the fact that the events it recounts really happened mean that it has often been classified as a record of the Second World War.

In the afterword he added to the book in 1998, Joffo explains why he did not write about his experiences until much later on. Like many of the writers who ended up sharing their experience of the conflict, he did not originally intend to describe what he had gone through, but the passage of time and the lingering trauma of his experiences led him to tell his story as part of an attempt to finally move on.

Joffo's decision to write this autobiography can be ascribed to a sort of duty to remember: by the time he wrote the novel, he had three children of his own, and he expresses a hope that they will never know the fear and suffering he experienced. He hopes that the events of the Holocaust will never be repeated, and believes that by passing his memories on to future generations, he can help ensure that they do not forget or fall into the same traps.

## Homage to the Righteous

As well as paying homage to Joffo's contemporaries and loved ones, *A Bag of Marbles* depicts French members of the "Righteous Among the Nations", the name given to non-Jews who risked their lives to save Jews during the Second World War.

In particular, he pays tribute to the French clergy, whose clandestine but highly effective actions greatly hindered the deportations, and to other citizens and members of the Resistance who helped him. These include:

- the priest who looked out for him and his brother in Dax and saved them from being arrested by the SS men who were patrolling the carriages and checking the passengers' identity papers;
- the priest at the church of La Buffa in Nice, who risks his life to provide fake baptism certificates and offers false testimony to secure the brothers' release;
- Subinagui, the director of New Harvest, who secretly harbours Jewish children in his Pétainist camp.

*A Bag of Marbles* is something of a testimony, as Joffo recounts his story against the backdrop of the difficult events of the Occupation. As well as remembering a dark period in European history, he pays homage to the victims of the war, and to the Righteous and the members of the Resistance, particularly those who helped him and his brother to survive the conflict.

# A CHILD'S-EYE VIEW OF THE WAR

*A Bag of Marbles* recounts Joffo's memories and his experiences as a ten-year-old boy during the war, which means that the story is told from a child's point of view.

## The theme of childhood

Although the novel is set during the war, many of the episodes it features are centred around universal childhood memories:

- The author describes the joys of childhood games. For example, the novel opens with a description of the two brothers' games of marbles in the playground. The book's title refers to the episode in which Joseph trades the yellow star he is forced to wear because he is Jewish for his friend Zérati's bag of marbles, thus sharply evoking the contrast between the horrors of the war and the boys' carefree childhood games. Later on, Joffo describes lively football matches on the beach at Menton, his sense of wonder as he discovers the magic of the cinema, the joy of his trips to the beach, and games of jacks.

- He also discusses his childhood friendships and memories from school, although the boys' schooling was interrupted by the war: he mentions going back to school, his "struggle with a geometry problem", his classmates, his lessons and "the last day of school, [when] prizes were distributed". He also describes his squabbles with Maurice, his friendship with Virgilio in Menton and his easy understanding with Ange at New Harvest.
- Finally, he recalls his first love, Françoise Mancelier, who at 14 was two years older than him. His impossible love for the daughter of a Pétainist bookshop owner who shelters Joseph in R. adds the final touches to his depiction of the war. As he himself writes, "If I hadn't had my love story during that period of flight, something would be missing from the picture".

## War as a game

In spite of the hardship Joseph faces during the war, as he is separated from his family and he and his loved ones are in constant danger, he often sees the situation as a kind of game. He finds enjoyment in his resourcefulness and, somewhat paradoxically, derives a sense of freedom from his family's oppression by the Nazis: "at our age, earning a living had become a wonderful game, one that was more interesting than soccer games on the beach or exploring deserted villas".

He also enjoys some carefree moments during these three difficult years. When they stop in Marseille during their first journey, the brothers see the day as "a great, riotous, windy festival – my most beautiful promenade". He is equally enthusiastic about his time in Menton, and compares his stay in Nice to a holiday: "if it weren't for the ritual of listening to Radio London each night, I'd swear we were spending a pleasant summer on the Côte d'Azur".

As such, in spite of the terrible events that form the backdrop to the novel, some of Joffo's memories evoke a carefree time and his descriptions are shaped by a child's point of view that contrasts with the pathos that often characterises books about the war and the Occupation.

## A coming-of-age novel

*A Bag of Marbles* can also be classified as a coming-of-age novel, meaning one which follows a character who overcomes a series of obstacles to complete a quest and attain happiness, often assisted by one or more other characters. In doing so, they experience moral, psychological and intellectual growth.

Joffo describes his book as "the story of two children in a world of cruelty, absurdity, and, at times, helpfulness of the most unexpected kind". They face a series of setbacks on their way, and the reader sees them grow and evolve over the course of the story. In the context of the Second World War, the goal of their quest is survival: they must stay alive until the end of the war.

As the story progresses Joffo grows up, becomes tougher and loses his childlike naivety. At the end of the novel, he reflects that the Nazis have stolen his childhood from him: "They haven't taken my life; they've done something worse – they've robbed me of my childhood. They've killed the child that I might have been". As the story ends, so does Joseph's childhood. When he returns home and catches a glimpse of his reflection in the window of his family's hair salon, he observes: "It's true, I've grown". These are the last words of the novel before the epilogue.

# A STORY OF HOPE AND FEAR

By sharing his testimony, Joffo does not intend to be just one more critic of Hitler's regime: he focuses on his experiences and the tragedy that accompanied them, but in spite of this, there is still a message of hope running through the novel. The narrative therefore comprises calmer periods punctuated by sudden tragic events, which reflects the novel's two central themes: hope and fear.

## Fear

When the two brothers leave Paris, they are thrust into a world where fear is a constant presence. They themselves are scared, as they do not know what will happen to them or what tomorrow will bring: "I have a curious feeling in my stomach: it's as if my intestines had suddenly become independent and wanted to get out of their bag of skin". There is also the fear linked to the anti-Semitic manhunt in France, as can be clearly seen when they are brutally arrested in Nice: "my brother doesn't have quite the same face as a little while ago. Maybe we'll never again have the faces we used to have".

Very early on, Maurice and Joseph decide to live each day as it comes and to improvise if things go wrong. Over time, as Joseph grows increasingly disillusioned and weary and experiences the myriad horrors of the war, he almost forgets about his fear: "Actually, I may not even care if I go on living... But the machine has been started up; the game must go on according to the rules. [...] I'll do everything I can to rob them of the pleasure of getting me".

## Hope

However, these tragic moments are interspersed with calmer periods when the children's life regains a sense of normality, allowing the two brothers to grow and thrive while enjoying a respite from the horrors of war. The idyllic nature of these lighter moments is accentuated by the fact that they always take place in sunny locations such as Marseille and Menton, where the brothers also discover new and exciting things (the cinema in Marseille, life in the mountains in Menton).

## The joy of the Liberation

Their hope is finally rewarded when peace returns at the end of the novel. After spending three years trying to outrun death, Joseph can hardly believe what is happening as his nightmare comes to an end: "[...] it was all over. I was free. Nobody was trying to kill me anymore. I could go back home, take trains, walk in the street, laugh, ring doorbells, play at marbles in the schoolyard on the rue Ferdinand-Flocon".

In his account of the Liberation, Joffo describes the general jubilation and intense feeling of relief, but also the punishments meted out to collaborationists. He is euphoric and wants nothing more than to be reunited with his loved ones and go back to his life as it was before the war. When the Resistance members in R. want him to stay in the village so that he can continue delivering newspapers and carrying messages, he tells them: "I left home three years ago. My family is scattered all over. Today I can go back, so I'm going. And you can't stop me".

He goes home to his old neighbourhood, the family's hair salon, Albert, Henri and his mother.

However, his relief and joy are marred by the discovery that his father is dead: "I also see that Papa isn't there; I understand that he will never be there anymore". Although the members of the Joffo family have been beaten down and permanently scarred by the war, they can finally start living again.

# **FURTHER REFLECTION**

## SOME QUESTIONS TO THINK ABOUT...

- To what extent can this autobiographical novel be described as a public service?
- In what ways can we say that writing the novel was a form of therapy for Joffo?
- What importance does the author place on the depiction of historical events in the novel, compared with the portrayal of his own experiences?
- In your opinion, to what extent were Joseph and his brother victims of Nazi oppression, even though they were not deported to a camp?
- In what ways do Joseph's travels through France constitute a coming-of-age journey?
- How does the novel illustrate the absurdity of anti-Semitism?
- This novel has been adapted for the cinema twice. In your opinion, was the novel or one of the films the most evocative? Justify your

answer.
- Do you think that all testimonies about the Second World War and the Holocaust can be adapted for the cinema? Consider in particular *The Human Race* (1947) by Robert Antelme (French writer, 1917-1990) and *If This is a Man* (1947) by Primo Levi (Italian writer, 1919-1987). Justify your answer.
- To what extent can *A Bag of Marbles* be described as an optimistic novel?

*We want to hear from you!*
*Leave a comment on your online library*
*and share your favourite books on social media!*

# FURTHER READING

## REFERENCE EDITION

- Joffo, J. (2001) *A Bag of Marbles*. Trans. Sokolinsky, M. Chicago: University of Chicago Press.

## ADAPTATIONS

- *A Bag of Marbles*. (1975) [Film]. Jacques Doillon. Dir. France: AMLF.
- *A Bag of Marbles*. (2017) [Film]. Christian Duguay. Dir. France/Canada/Czech Republic: Quad Productions, Main Journey.

# Bright ≡Summaries.com

## More guides to rediscover your love of literature

- **Animal Farm** by George Orwell
- **The Stranger** by Albert Camus
- **Harry Potter and the Sorcerer's Stone** by J.K. Rowling
- **The Silence of the Sea** by Vercors
- **Antigone** by Jean Anouilh
- **The Flowers of Evil** by Baudelaire

www.brightsummaries.com

Although the editor makes every effort to verify the accuracy of the information published, BrightSummaries.com accepts no responsibility for the content of this book.

**© BrightSummaries.com, 2018. All rights reserved.**

www.brightsummaries.com

Ebook EAN: 9782806270443

Paperback EAN: 9782806274014

Legal Deposit: D/2015/12603/613

This guide was written with the collaboration of Margot Pépin and translated with the collaboration of Rebecca Neal for the character study of Henri and Albert Joffo and of the parents, and for the sections "The autobiographical pact", "A child's-eye view of the war" and "The joy of the Liberation".

Cover: © Primento

Digital conception by Primento, the digital partner of publishers.

Printed in Great Britain
by Amazon